English Skills

2

Writing
and
Vocabulary

John Barwick
Jenny Barwick

OXFORD
UNIVERSITY PRESS

Introduction

The *English Skills* series is designed to promote and support the development of a high standard of English language use, an essential asset for academic success, and success in the world beyond school.

The series contains two strands:

> *Writing and Vocabulary* (Books 1–3)
> *Writing and Grammar* (Books 1–3)

The books provide teachers with a comprehensive program in English skills, and are also suitable for home use. A pull-out answer section is located in the middle of the book.

In keeping with the recent renewed emphasis on the explicit teaching of language and grammar skills, this series provides coverage of English skills in reading and writing, grammar and vocabulary, spelling and punctuation.

Writing and Vocabulary focuses on essential spelling rules, vocabulary content, and writing skills to provide a strong foundation for successful academic writing. There are a wide variety of activity types and all activities have the following goals:

GOAL   Develop and reinforce knowledge and recall of basic spelling rules and letter patterns

GOAL   Provide practice in useful spelling strategies

GOAL   Build vocabulary knowledge and recall

GOAL   Promote student confidence and independent work

Many activities incorporate content from curriculum areas such as mathematics, social studies, and the natural world.

Contents

For **plurals** of most words just add "s".	
Singular	**Plural**
one **forest**	several **forests**
one **nurse**	ten **nurses**

1 Write the plurals of the words.

one hook/four .... *hooks* ....

one cousin/five ....

one vegetable/a box of ....

one cupboard/two ....

one reason/many ....

one sentence/two ....

one pattern/several ....

one adventure/lots of ....

one mistake/many ....

one arrow/a few ....

one ankle/two ....

one uncle/a lot of ....

one friend/many ....

one answer/all the ....

one bounce/several ....

one guest/many ....

one castle/three ....

one blanket/two thick ....

2 Complete the sentences with plurals.

a (month) Each season has three.......... *months* ....

b (piece) My mother cut the cake into eight ....

c (blanket) I have three .... on my bed in winter.

d (Eagle) I saw three .... flying near my house.

e (building, shadow) The tall .... cast long ....

f (storm, winter) The coast has had five big .... during the last three ....

Unit 2

Letter patterns 1

English has many common letter patterns. Many English words have the letter pattern "ea".

1 Circle all the words with the letter pattern "ea".

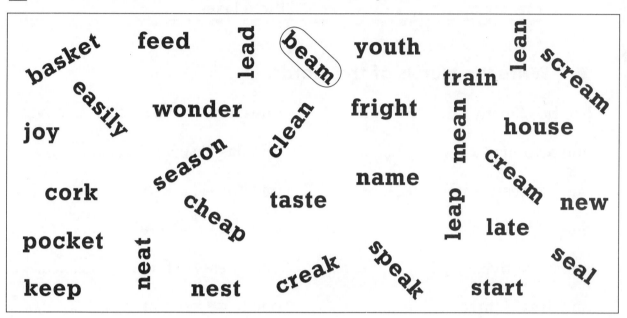

basket feed lead beam youth lean scream

easily wonder clean fright train mean house

joy season name leap cream new

cork cheap taste late seal

pocket neat name speak

keep nest creak start

2 Choose the correct "ea" word to complete the sentences.

~~leak~~ reason heat team eagle reach

a No matter how hard they looked, Jess and Aaron

could not find the...........*leak*........... in the container.

b The .... circled slowly overhead.

c Sam's .... for being late was that she had missed the bus.

d Dad was not tall enough to ....
the oranges on the tree.

e My .... came fifth in the competition.

f There was no .... in the old house.

3

| For **plurals** of words ending in "s", "ss", "x", or "z", add "es". ||
Singular	Plural
one **gas**	many types of **gases**
one **tax**	three **taxes**

1 Write the plurals of the words.

one bus / many .... _buses_ ....   one circus / two ....

one octopus / a few ....   one pass / several ....

one address / a book of ....   one box / a pile of..............................

one waltz / three ....   one cross / several..............................

one loss / five................................   one guess / a few..................................

one dress / three............................   one toss / several..................................

one boss / too many........................   one miss / three bad..............................

2 Complete the sentences with plurals.

a (fox) We saw three .... _foxes_ .... in the field.

b (mailbox) The mailman put the letters in all the ....

c (eyewitness) There were several .... to the robbery.

d (glass) The .... broke when Roberto dropped the box.

e (compass) The campers used .... to find their way
   out of the forest.

Unit 4

Homophones are words that sound the same, but have different spellings and different meanings.	
Sun/son	The **sun** disappeared behind the clouds. My uncle's **son** is my cousin.
hear/here	Can you **hear** the train coming? Your coat is right over **here**.

1 **Choose the correct word to complete the sentences.**

a (cent/scent/sent) "I........<u>sent</u>.......... the letter last week," said Hisako.

b (cent/scent/sent) A one-........................ coin is called a penny in the USA.

c (cent/scent/sent) The .... of perfume is easy to smell.

d (rain/rein/reign) London gets a lot of .... every year.

e (rain/rein/reign) The .... of Queen Elizabeth II began in 1954.

f (rain/rein/reign) She pulled on the .... to make the horse slow down.

g (hangar/hanger) There's a .... in the closet for your coat.

h (hangar/hanger) There are three airplanes in the ....

i (new/knew) Bae-yong was the only person who .... the answer.

j (new/knew) "I have a .... bike," shouted Zac.

k (threw/through) Jackie peeked .... a gap in the fence.

Writing

2 **Rewrite the sentences with all words spelled correctly.**

a I reterned that book last weak.

....

b Su-jin is meating me befor the game.

....

Singular	Plural
one **lunch**	two **lunches**
one **crash**	three **crashes**

For **plurals** of words ending in "ch" or "sh", add "es".

1   Write the plurals of the words.

one eyelash / all my ....*eyelashes*....   one clash / several ....

one sandwich / two ....   one dish / a stack of ....

one splash / three ....   one match / two great ....

one peach / a box of.........................   one beach / many ....

one branch / a few ....   one push / three big...........................

one flash / many bright.....................   one wish / three ....

2   Complete the sentences with plurals.

a   (paintbrush) Mani cleaned the....*paintbrushes*.... after the lesson.

b   (match) I watched two tennis .... on TV yesterday.

c   (radish) We grew some .... in our vegetable garden.

d   (watch) Remember to take your .... off before
you go swimming.

e   (switch) There are four light .... in the living room.

Unit 6

Find the number words in the box. Write the words as you find them.

eleven	twelve	thirteen	~~fourteen~~	fifteen	sixteen	seventeen
eighteen	nineteen	twenty	thirty	forty	fifty	sixty
seventy	eighty	ninety	hundred	thousand	zero	

```
n i n e t e e n f i f t e n
n t e t w e l s i x t e e n
e l e v e n t i f o r t y y
e d z s l a z x t w e n t y
t n s e v e n t y e n t y y
h a s v e t t y t h g i e t
g s e e n t y o r t y e z e
i u v n e w t f i f t e e n
e o e t h i r t h i r t r i
v h n e t h i r t e e n o n
e t n e e t r u o f o u r t
n h u n d r e d a s u o h t
```

.............fourteen............. ....

....

....

....

....

....

....

....

Unit 7

For **plurals** of words ending in "ay", "ey", or "oy", add "s".	
Singular	**Plural**
one **day**	two **days**
one **key**	three **keys**
one **toy**	a lot of **toys**

1 **Write the plurals of the words.**

one guy / three ....guys...............   one bay / two wide ....

one donkey / two white.....................   one birthday / four ....

one highway / several ....   one day / six...

one spray / a few.............................   one alley / four ....

one valley / many ....   one chimney / three smoking ....

one journey / several ....   one freeway / two ....

2 **Complete the sentences with plurals.**

a (tray) There are a lot of......trays........ in the lunch room.

b (volley) In volleyball, a team can do two .... before returning the ball over the net.

c (monkey) I saw about 20 .... at the zoo.

d (holiday) Christmas and New Year's Eve are big .... in many countries.

e (boy, key) Some .... found the .... behind the chair.

Unit 8

English has many common letter patterns. Many English words begin with the letter pattern "fl".

1 Circle all the words with the letter pattern "fl".

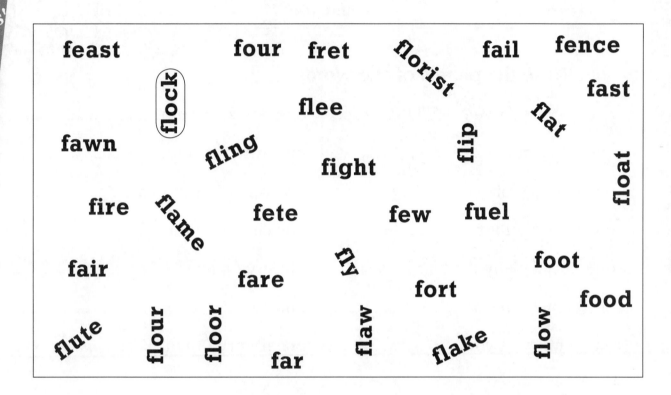

feast   four   fret   florist   fail   fence

flock   flee   flip   flat   fast

fawn   fling   fight   float

fire   flame   fete   few   fuel

fair   fly   foot

fare   fort   food

flute   flour   floor   far   flaw   flake   flow

2 Choose the correct "fl" word to complete the sentences.

> flood   flap   flat   flash   flavor   ~~fleet~~

a   The.......*fleet*.......... of ships sailed out of the harbor.

b   Many people ran away as the .... waters rose quickly.

c   This ice cream is my favorite ....

d   A .... of lightning hit the tree near my house.

e   There are no hills in the town – it's completely ....

f   We have a .... in our back door so our cat can get in and out of the house.

Unit 9

For **plurals** of words ending in a consonant followed by "y", change the "y" to "i" and add "es".

Singular	Plural
one **family**	several **families**
one **ferry**	three **ferries**

1 **Write the plurals of the words.**

one country / five ....*countries*.......   one dairy / several ....

one jury / most ....   one army / many ....

one hobby / lots of ....   one reply / three...............................

one factory / four ....   one city / several ....

one duty / many..................................   one cry / a few ....

one baby / three..................................   one battery / two ....

one century / two...............................   one library / many ....

2 **Complete the sentences with plurals.**

a (try) Matt took three ....*tries*........ to blow out the candles on his birthday cake.

b (trophy) I have five .... on my bookshelf.

c (entry) There are 50 .... for the contest.

d (story) The building is over 20 .... high.

There are seven days of the week. They are named after different things.

1 **Match the days of the week to their meanings.**

This day is named after the Viking god of thunder, Thor   Monday

This day is named after the planet Saturn   Tuesday

This day is named after the moon   Wednesday

This day is named after the Viking god of war, Tiw   Thursday

This day is named after Thor's wife, Frigga   Friday

This day is named after the king of the gods, Woden   Saturday

This day is named after the sun   Sunday

2 **Put six days of the week in the correct rows. Another day of the week will appear in the shaded column.**

	T	H	U	R	S	D	A	Y	
						E			Y
			M			A			
		A							
		N	S						
			I						

The day in the shaded column is ....

For **plurals** of some words ending in "f" or "fe", change the "f" to "v" and add "es".	
Singular	**Plural**
one **wolf**	a pack of **wolves**
one **leaf**	many **leaves**

1 Write the plurals of the words.

one leaf / a pile of ......*leaves*...........   one wife / three...................................

one life / many................................   yourself / ....

one calf / five ....   one thief / a gang of ....

one shelf / four ....   one half / two.....................................

For **plurals** of some words ending in "f" or "fe", add "s".	
Singular	**Plural**
one **gulf**	three **gulfs**
one **puff**	four **puffs**

2 Write the plurals of the words.

one gulf / three ....*gulfs*...........   one chief / five ....

one puff / several ....   one reef / three...................................

one giraffe / a couple of ....   one cliff / two.....................................

one cuff / two................................   one safe / three locked ....

For **plurals** of some words ending in "f" or "fe", it can be done **both ways**. Your choice!	
Singular	**Plural**
one **dwarf**	a group of **dwarves**
	a group of **dwarfs**

3 Write both plural forms of the words.

one dwarf / a few *dwarfs dwarves* one hoof / four ....

one staff / two ....   one scarf / three long ....

Follow the steps below to practice spelling new and difficult words.

Look carefully at the word.

Say the word and **listen** as you say it.

Cover the word with something.

Write the word.

Check your spelling.

Practice spelling the words.

color	*color*	country	
beginning		guess	
although		biscuit	
library		weigh	
easy		famous	
friend		certain	
caught		answer	
tongue		building	
library		forty	
piece		healthy	
enough		except	
favorite		already	
among		daughter	
careful		beautiful	
breakfast		guest	

For **plurals** of some words ending in "o", add "es."	
Singular	**Plural**
one **volcano**	two **volcanoes**
one **potato**	a bag of **potatoes**

1 Write the plurals of the words.

one potato / a bag of ......*potatoes*......   one tornado / a few wild ....

one tomato / a box of ....   one hero / two.............................

one mango / six ....   one mosquito / three ....

For **plurals** of some words ending in "o", add "s".	
Singular	**Plural**
one **kangaroo**	three **kangaroos**
one **piano**	three **pianos**

2 Write the plurals of the words.

one piano / two ....*pianos*..........   one radio / several ....

one video / lots of ....   one zero / three ....

one zoo / two ....   one photo / an album of.......................

one rodeo / a few ....   one stereo / a shop full of ....

3 Complete the sentences with plurals.

a (potato) The bag of....*potatoes*..... was very heavy.

b (zero) There are two .... in 100.

c (piano) This piece of music was written for two ....

d (mosquito) There were hundreds of .... in the tent.

e (tomato) My grandfather grows .... in summer.

14

> **Synonyms** are words with the same or similar meanings.
>
> **Right** and **correct** are synonyms. They have the same meaning.
>
> **Hat** and **cap** are synonyms too.

1   **Match the words with their synonyms.**

space	scrape	spark	prison	estimate	~~forest~~
		jump	message		

woods ....*forest*.............   jail ....

gap ....   guess ....

flash ....   leap ....

scratch ....   note ....

> **Antonyms** are words with opposite meanings.
>
> **Right** and **wrong** are antonyms. They have opposite meanings.
>
> **Stand up** and **sit down** are antonyms too.

2   **Match the words with their antonyms.**

true	rich	behind	worse	receive	sell	cheap
		before	~~male~~	ask		

female ....*male*.............   dear ....

ahead ....   better ....

buy ....   give ....

afterwards ....   poor ....

false ....   answer ....

For some **irregular plurals**, change some letters in the word's singular form.	
one **man**	four **men**
one **mouse**	two **mice**

1   Write the plurals of the words.

one mouse / six.............*mice*.................   one foot / both ....

one tooth / three of my ....   one woman / a group of ....

one ox / six...   one child / many ....

Some **irregular plurals** have the same form as the singular.	
one **trout**	four **trout**
one **sheep**	two **sheep**

2   Write the correct plurals of the words.

one sheep / a flock of.....................*sheep*.........................

one deer / a herd of ....

one pair of tweezers / a box full of ....

one salmon / a school of ....

3   Write the correct plurals of the words.

clothes / clotheses ....*clothes*............   sheep / sheeps...................................

womans / women ....   teeth / toothes ....

gooses / geese ....   trout / trouts.....................................

mouses / mice..................................   oxes / oxen.......................................

childs / children ....   mans / men.......................................

foots / feet......................................   deers / deer ....

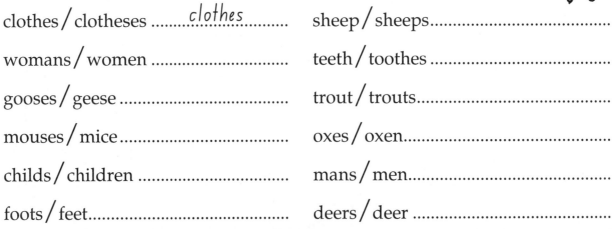

Unit 16

English has many common letter patterns. Many English words have the letter pattern "ch".

1 Circle all the words with the letter pattern "ch".

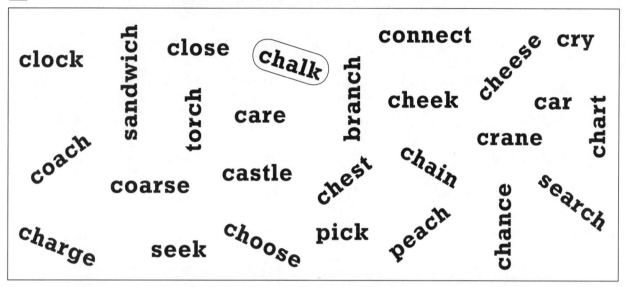

clock sandwich close (chalk) connect cheese cry

branch cheek car chart

torch care crane

coach castle chest chain

coarse search

charge seek choose pick peach chance

2 Choose the correct "ch" word to complete the sentences.

> bunch   cherries   check   chair   ~~cheap~~

a My bike was very........*cheap*........ because it was second-hand.

b We bought a .... of flowers for my grandmother.

c Make sure you sit properly on the ....

d .... are my favorite fruit.

e "....................... your answers before you hand in your books," advised Mr. Poulos.

Test your plural power!

Write the correct plural forms.

sentryes / sentries...........*sentries*........

geese / gooses ....

chimnies / chimneys.............................

matches / matchs..................................

eagls / eagles..

gulfs / gulves ....

tomatos / tomatoes ....

wifes / wives ....

highways / highwayes ....

oxen / oxes ....

monkies / monkeys..............................

factoryes / factories.............................

pianoes / pianos....................................

piecs / pieces ....

answeres / answers...............................

giraffes / giraffs ....

guests / guestes ....

answeres / answers...............................

shelves / shelfs......................................

clashes / clash's....................................

cross's / crosses.....................................

friendes / friends ....

replys / replies ....

peachs / peaches....................................

chieves / chiefs......................................

bushs / bushes ....

waltzs / waltzes.....................................

trophys / trophies..................................

entryes / entries.....................................

videoes / videos.....................................

sandwiches / sandwichs ....

knifes / knives.......................................

castles / castls..

handes / hands ....

Look out, we have guests!

Homophones are words that sound the same, but have different spellings and different meanings.	
no/know	There's **no** juice in the fridge. **I know** the answer.
ate/eight	**I ate** two sandwiches. The boy is **eight** years old.

1 Choose the correct word to complete the sentences.

a (pour/poor) There are a lot of......*poor*....... people in the world.

b (pour/poor) Be careful when you .... the hot water.

c (weigh/way) This is the .... to the library.

d (weigh/way) The suitcases each .... about 30 kilograms.

e (allowed/aloud) Chewing gum isn't .... in school.

f (allowed/aloud) Makoto read the story .... to his little brother.

g (peace/piece) The two countries signed a .... agreement to end the war.

h (peace/piece) I'd like a .... of cake with strawberries.

i (creak/creek) I walked in the .... and my feet got wet.

j (creak/creek) The old door opened with a loud ....

Writing

2 Rewrite the sentences with all words spelled correctly.

a I have a blister on the heal of my foot.

....

b Our feet wer very soar after our long walk.

....

Present tense verbs
For many verbs in the present tense, add "s" when used after **he** or **she**.

I decide	He/She **decides**
print	**prints**

1 Add "s" to the following verbs.

print ....*prints*............   rake ....

drill ....   toast ....

receive ....   skate ....

steal ....   report ....

waste ....   notice ....

answer ....   manage ....

guard ....   arrive ....

2 Add "s" to the following verbs.

a (explain) This book...*explains*.... how cars work.

b (shine) The sun .... in my window every morning in summer.

c (swim) Peter .... every week.

d (speak) My neighbor .... English, and French.

e (forget) Joel often .... to bring his textbooks.

Find the space words in the box. Write the words as you find them.

graph	column	category	backwards	~~forwards~~	direction	flip
slide	turn	hexagon	octagon	pentagon	rectangle	parallel
		pyramid	prism			

s	u	b	m	o	h	r	m	a	r	g	n	a	t
p	e	n	t	a	g	o	n	m	s	l	i	d	e
a	a	c	a	t	e	g	o	r	y	n	d	i	s
c	o	r	u	o	s	i	g	i	r	w	i	m	s
t	w	r	g	w	d	w	a	u	h	p	r	a	e
a	h	w	a	r	r	a	t	h	o	a	e	r	l
l	e	l	g	n	a	t	c	e	r	r	c	y	l
l	x	e	p	a	w	p	o	x	h	a	t	p	a
y	a	p	p	y	k	u	h	a	o	l	i	r	t
m	g	u	r	u	c	e	w	g	m	l	o	i	i
a	o	s	d	r	a	w	r	o	f	e	n	s	o
r	n	y	w	t	b	e	e	c	o	l	u	m	n

................forwards................   ....

....

....

....

....

....

....

....

Present tense verbs
To describe an action that happens **now**, use "am", "is", or "are", then add "ing".
I boil water. **I am boiling** water.
She drills a hole. She **is drilling** a hole.

1 Add "ing" to the following verbs.

boil ....*boiling*......... do ....

guard .... guess ....

shift .... mark ....

stamp .... creak ....

crawl .... explain ....

wonder .... allow ....

comfort .... weigh ....

scream .... answer ....

crowd .... shout ....

accept .... bring ....

2 Add "ing" to the following verbs.

a (coach) Joel's father is...*coaching*.. us this year.

b (depart) The train is .... in three minutes.

c (load) The crane is .... the containers onto the vessel.

d (lead) Gemma was .... the race as the runners came into view.

e (butter) Zeke is .... the bread.

f (gather) We are .... berries.

English has many common letter patterns. Many English words have the letter pattern "igh".

1 Circle all the words with the letter pattern "igh".

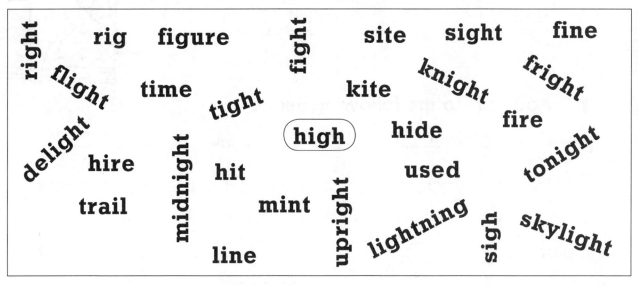

right   rig   figure   fight   site   sight   fine

flight   time   tight   kite   knight   fright

delight   hire   midnight   hit   high   hide   fire

trail   mint   used   tonight

line   upright   lightning   sigh   skylight

2 Choose the correct "igh" word.

night   tight   lights   brightly   ~~might~~   slight   thighs

a   I ....*might*.....be able to come to your house after school.

b   Jack is okay. He only has a .... cut on his arm.

c   These pants are too small. They're too .... around my waist.

d   At .... we can see the city .... in the distance.

e   The gold coins were shining .... in the sun.

f   The water came up to my ....

Verb endings 3

Past tense verbs	
For many verbs, simply add "ed".	
groan	**groaned**
drill	**drilled**

1 Add "ed" to the following verbs.

groan ......*groaned*......   hook ....

shower ....   sail ....

guess ....   address ....

appear ....   scratch ....

connect ....   chain ....

accept ....   bloom ....

blend ....   answer ....

smash ....   discuss ....

lift ....   sigh ....

2 Add "ed" to the following verbs.

a (shift) Its load....*shifted*..... as the truck went around the sharp corner.

b (doubt) I .... the story, but Jee-hyun believed it.

c (guard) Three men .... the entrance to the bank.

d (calm) The water .... as the wind dropped.

e (stain) The juice from the berries .... Tadashi's white shirt.

f (explain) The attendant .... how the machine worked.

Mammals are animals with hair or fur. They breathe air.

Birds are animals that have feathers. Most birds can fly.

Fish are animals that live in the water. They breathe underwater.

Reptiles are animals without hair or fur. They have skin like leather.

Write the words in the box in the correct list.

eagle ~~wolf~~ shark deer turtle piranha hawk
kangaroo salmon penguin trout crocodile
owl lizard lion carp sanke sparrow

Mammals	Birds	Fish	Reptiles
wolf	eagle	shark	turtle

Present tense verbs	
For verbs ending in silent "e", drop the "e" and add "ing" for actions happening **now**.	
dare	He's **daring** me to do it.
escape	The bird is **escaping** form the cage.

1 Add "ing" to the following verbs.

dare	.............daring.........	score	....
shine	....	charge	....
receive	....	bake	....
rate	....	serve	....
rescue	....	damage	....
compare	....	manage	....
hope	....	serve	....
escape	....	promise	....

2 Add "ing" to the following verbs.

a   (become) It was ...becoming... dark so we went inside.

b   (compete) I am .... in three races today.

c   (solve) Su-hee is very good at .... puzzles.

d   (stage) My class is .... a play next week.

e   (write) I am .... a letter to my grandfather.

These chunks will make a great milkshake!

Syllables		
Breaking up words into chunks can help you spell and pronounce them correctly.		
One syllable	**Two syllables**	**Three syllables**
serve	become (be-come)	seventy (se-ven-ty)
get	allow (al-low)	magnify (mag-ni-fy)
mark	closet (clo-set)	blueberry (blue-ber-ry)

Put the words from the box in the correct list.

~~manage~~ ~~sound~~ ~~subtraction~~ common although score
anywhere favorite mass capital famous library mistake
fruit adventure cupboard cream guest surprise
commencing flight however matter weigh healthy youth
building afternoon taste carefully

One-syllable words	Two-syllable words	Three-syllable words
sound	*manage*	*subtraction*
....	....	....
....	....	....
....	....	....
....	....	....
....	....	....
....	....	....
....	....	....
....	....	....

Past tense verbs	
For verbs ending with a silent "e", drop the "e" and add "ed".	
promise	She **promised** to help me.
score	He **scored** two goals in the soccer game yesterday.

1   Add "ed" to the following verbs.

bore ....*bored*........... face ....

rage .... taste ....

prepare .... notice ....

charge .... serve ....

waste .... compete ....

manage .... double ....

solve .... rate ....

bounce .... bake ....

2   Add "ed" to the following verbs.

a   (sense) The horses.....*sensed*..... the danger.

b   (tangle) Our fishing lines were hopelessly ....

c   (arrange) I .... to meet Nim outside the pool.

d   (rescue) Several sailors were .... from the sea after their ship sank.

e   (receive) I .... three presents on my birthday.

f   (sneeze) I .... many times yesterday because I had a bad cold.

Answers

Unit 1

1 hooks, arrows, cousins, ankles, vegetables, uncles, cupboards, friends, reasons, answers, sentences, bounces, patterns, guests, adventures, castles, mistakes, blankets

2 a months **b** pieces **c** blankets **d** Eagles **e** buildings, shadows **f** storms, winters

Unit 2

1 lead, lean, clean, easily, scream, mean, beam, cheap, season, cream, creak, leap, neat, speak, seal

2 a leak **b** eagle **c** reason **d** reach **e** team **f** heat

Unit 3

1 buses, circuses, octopuses, passes, addresses, boxes, waltzes, crosses, losses, guesses, dresses, tosses, bosses, misses

2 a foxes **b** mailboxes **c** eyewitnesses **d** glasses **e** compasses

Unit 4

1 a sent **b** cent **c** scent **d** Rain **e** reign **f** rein **g** hanger **h** hangar **i** knew **j** new **k** through

2 a I returned that book last week. **b** Su-jin is meeting me before the game.

Unit 5

1 eyelashes, clashes, sandwiches, dishes, splashes, matches, peaches, beaches, branches, pushes, flashes, wishes

2 a paintbrushes **b** matches **c** radishes **d** watches **e** switches

Unit 6

Unit 7

1 guys, bays, donkeys, birthdays, highways, days, sprays, alleys, valleys, chimneys, journeys, freeways

2 a trays **b** volleys **c** monkeys **d** holidays **e** boys, keys

Unit 8

1 flock, flip, flat, florist, flee, flour, fling, flame, fly, flute, flaw, flow, float, floor, flake

2 a fleet **b** flood **c** flavor **d** flash **e** flat **f** flap

Unit 9

1 countries, dairies, juries, armies, hobbies, replies, factories, cities, duties, cries, babies, batteries, centuries, libraries

2 a tries **b** trophies **c** entries **d** stories

Unit 10

1 Monday—the moon; Tuesday—Tiw; Wednesday—Woden; Thursday—Thor; Friday—Frigga; Saturday—the planet Saturn; Sunday—the sun

2

Unit 11

1 leaves, wives, lives, yourselves, calves, thieves, shelves, halves

2 gulfs, chiefs, puffs, reefs, giraffes, cliffs, cuffs, safes

3 dwarfs, dwarves; hoofs, hooves; staffs, staves; scarfs, scarves

Unit 12

(check that all words are spelled correctly)

Unit 13

1 potatoes, tornadoes, tomatoes, heroes, mangoes, mosquitoes

2 pianos, radios, videos, zeros, zoos, photos, rodeos, stereos

3 a potatoes **b** zeros **c** pianos **d** mosquitoes **e** tomatoes

Unit 14

1 forest, prison, space, estimate, spark, jump, scrape, message

2 male, cheap, behind, worse, sell, receive, before, rich, true, ask

Unit 15

1 mice, feet, teeth, women, oxen, children.

2 sheep, deer, tweezers, salmon

3 clothes, sheep, women, teeth, geese, trout, mice, oxen, children, men, feet, deer

Answers

Unit 16

1 sandwich, chalk, branch, cheese, coach, chest, cheek, charge, torch, chain chart, chance, choose, peach, search

2 a cheap **b** bunch **c** chair **d** Cherries **e** Check

Unit 17

sentries, answers, geese, shelves, chimneys, clashes, matches, crosses, eagles, friends, gulfs, replies, tomatoes, peaches, wives, chiefs, highways, bushes, oxen, waltzes, monkies, trophies, factories, entries, pianos, videos, pieces, sandwiches, answers, knives, giraffes, castles, guests, hands

Unit 18

1 a poor **b** pour **c** way **d** weigh **e** allowed **f** aloud **g** peace **h** piece **i** creek **j** creak

2 a I have a blister on the heel of my foot.
b Our feet were very sore after our long walk.

Unit 19

1 prints, rakes, drills, toasts, receives, skates, steals, reports, wastes, notices, answers, manages, guards, arrives

2 a explains **b** shines **c** swims **d** speaks **e** forgets

Unit 20

s	u	b	m	o	h	r	m	a	r	g	n	a	t
p	e	n	t	a	g	o	n	m	s	l	i	d	e
a	a	c	a	t	e	g	o	r	y	n	d	i	s
c	o	r	u	o	s	i	g	i	r	w	i	m	s
t	w	r	g	w	d	w	a	u	h	p	r	a	e
a	h	w	a	r	r	a	t	h	o	a	e	r	l
l	e	l	g	n	a	t	c	e	r	r	c	y	l
l	x	e	p	a	w	p	o	x	h	a	t	p	a
y	a	p	p	y	k	u	h	a	o	l	i	r	t
m	g	u	r	u	c	e	w	g	m	l	o	i	i
a	o	s	d	r	a	w	r	o	f	e	n	s	o
r	n	y	w	t	b	e	e	c	o	l	u	m	n

Unit 21

1 boiling, doing, guarding, guessing, shifting, marking, stamping, creaking, crawling, explaining, wondering, allowing, comforting, weighing, screaming, answering, crowding, shouting, accepting, bringing

2 a coaching **b** departing **c** loading **d** leading **e** buttering **f** gathering

Unit 22

1 right, flight, fright, fight, tight, delight, sight, knight, high, sigh, tonight, midnight, upright, skylight, lightning

2 a might **b** slight **c** tight **d** night, lights **e** brightly **f** thighs

Unit 23

1 groaned, hooked, showered, sailed, guessed, addressed, appeared, scratched, connected, chained, accepted, bloomed, blended, answered, smashed, discussed, lifted, sighed

2 a shifted **b** doubted **c** guarded **d** calmed **e** stained **f** explained

Unit 24

Mammals — wolf, deer, kangaroo, lion, horse
Birds — eagle, hawk, penguin, owl, sparrow
Fish — shark, piranha, salmon, trout, carp
Reptiles — turtle, crocodile, lizard, snake

Unit 25

1 daring, scoring, shining, charging, receiving, baking, rating, serving, rescuing, damaging, comparing, managing, hoping, serving, escaping, promising

2 a becoming **b** competing **c** solving **d** staging **e** writing

Unit 26

one-syllable words: sound, score, mass, fruit, cream, guest, flight, weigh, youth, taste; **two-syllable words:** manage, common, although, famous, mistake, cupboard, surprise, matter, healthy, building; **three-syllable words:** subtraction, anywhere, favorite, capital, library, adventure, commencing, however, afternoon, carefully

Unit 27

1 bored, faced, raged, tasted, prepared, noticed, charged, served, wasted, competed, managed, doubled, solved, rated, bounced, baked

2 a sensed **b** tangled **c** arranged **d** rescued **e** received **f** sneezed

Unit 28

1 mistake, rage, begin, bitter, slope, calm, course, hurt, tear, hop

2 first, forget, cruel, full, tight, waste, smooth, silent, build, hasty

Unit 29

1 spying, staying, obeying, marrying, spraying, straying, replying, frying, praying, burying, studying, hurrying, annoying, destroying, worrying, holidaying, enjoying, relaying

2 a supplying **b** delaying **c** hurrying **d** relying **e** carrying **f** displaying

11

Answers

Unit 30

1 crowd, crawl, crown, cradle, crease, cream, crackle cruel, crust, crime, crumb, creep, crush, crest, creature

2 a cramped **b** Crickets **c** crash **d** cruise **e** cross **f** crew

Unit 31

1 annoys, annoyed; destroys, destroyed; holidays, holidayed; relays, relayed; delays, delayed

2 dries, dried; tidies, tidied; replies, replied; studies, studied; empties, emptied; supplies, supplied

Unit 32

1 a sure **b** shore **c** missed **d** mist **e** plain **f** plane **g** waste **h** waist **i** weather **j** whether **k** It's **l** its

2 a We had a great time at the beach on Thursday.
b Adam collected the mail from the mailbox.

Unit 33

grabbed, grabbing; planned, planning; stripped, stripping; tripped, tripping; chopped, chopping; chatted, chatting; plugged, plugging; starred, starring; scrubbed, scrubbing; clipped, clipping; wrapped, wrapping; hugged, hugging

Unit 34

m	y	r	a	d	n	u	o	b	m	m	o	z	p
s	i	z	e	m	c	m	o	a	s	c	a	l	e
l	h	m	e	l	o	i	c	l	p	a	s	a	r
c	h	a	m	y	l	j	e	a	t	p	u	q	i
h	e	r	p	i	u	a	n	n	c	a	r	r	m
e	a	u	n	e	m	o	t	c	b	c	f	g	e
c	v	g	e	p	n	m	i	e	e	i	a	t	t
k	i	l	o	g	r	a	m	l	p	t	c	m	e
r	e	t	h	g	i	l	e	a	o	y	e	n	r
l	r	e	c	o	r	d	t	b	j	s	m	l	o
z	m	w	c	r	f	r	e	e	z	i	n	g	v
r	e	l	l	a	m	s	r	l	l	o	m	k	m

Unit 35

scratched, scratches, scratching; starred, stars, starring; buried, buries, burying; decided, decides, deciding; received, receives, receiving; replied, replies, replying; plugged, plugs, plugging; annoyed, annoys, annoying; wasted, wastes, wasting; answered, answers, answering; studied, studies, studying; guessed, guesses, guessing; clipped, clips, clipping; connected, connects, connecting; pedaled, pedals, pedaling; accompanied, accompanies, accompanying

Unit 36

1 toil, rejoice, spoil, boil, coil, join, choice, moist, soil, oil, poison, recoil, turquoise, noisy, avoid

2 a foiled **b** voice **c** point **d** noise **e** coins
f hoisted

Unit 37

1 floury, bossy, buttery, creamy, stormy, fruity, oily, shadowy, sugary, tricky, cloudy, misty

2 shiny, smoky, juicy, scary, shady, bouncy, rosy, wavy, tasty, stony, nosy, noisy, bony, stony

Unit 38

Z	S	E	R	R	O	T	J	A	N	S	Z	H	C
N	K	U	G	L	J	S	H	I	P	S	M	A	O
J	C	R	E	R	O	L	P	X	E	W	L	R	N
A	O	O	R	O	U	T	E	O	G	H	A	T	V
R	L	P	O	M	R	A	T	I	O	N	S	O	I
O	O	E	M	K	N	Z	M	L	E	A	Y	G	C
N	N	J	T	E	E	L	F	N	V	M	D	N	T
R	Y	W	V	O	Y	A	G	E	C	S	N	D	M
E	M	R	E	I	D	L	O	S	O	A	E	I	A
V	P	M	P	H	A	J	K	W	M	T	Y	A	S
O	T	R	A	N	S	P	O	R	T	E	D	R	T
G	W	P	D	P	H	I	L	L	I	P	I	Y	S

Unit 39

1 chatty, funny, knotty, smoggy, gassy, furry, sunny, scrubby

2 swimmer, drummer, wrapper, snapper, planner, stopper, hitter, tapper, cutter, winner, beginner, scanner, spinner, runner

Unit 40

Cities — Tokyo, Paris, Seoul, Sao Paolo, Los Angeles
Countries — Italy, Mexico, Canada, Korea, Thailand
Continents — Asia, North America, Europe, South America, Africa

Unit 41

shadier, shadiest; dustier, dustiest; healthier, healthiest; drier, driest; creamier, creamiest; oilier, oiliest; cloudier, cloudiest; heavier, heaviest; easier, easiest; livelier, liveliest; smoggier, smoggiest; noisier, noisiest; scarier, scariest

Unit 42

1 crush, grab, firm, guard, plot, knob, soil, crawl, castle, annoy

2 sick, ugly, apart, always, fancy, commence, gain, active, many, lead

Unit 43

1 calmly, surely, proudly, peacefully, tightly, kindly, hopefully, narrowly, famously, finally, commonly, friendly, strangely, purely, secretly, falsely, silently, cheaply

2 a blindly **b** smoothly **b** silently **b** quietly **e** usually

Answers

Unit 44

1 sound, loud, flour, hour, ground, amount, count, sour, aloud, announce, found, pounce, recount, clout, about

2 a bound **b** cloud **c** mouth **d** around **e** bounced

Unit 45

1 spoonful, pocketful, wasteful, successful, thoughtful, delightful, harmful, peaceful, careful, basketful, sinful, masterful, restful, youthful, doubtful, tearful

2 a painful **b** useful **c** helpful **d** playful **e** wonderful **f** mouthful

Unit 46

1 a hole **b** whole **c** hour **d** our **e** hoarse **f** horse **g** right **h** write **i** there **j** their

2 a How much is the fare to Seoul? **b** May I have some ice cream, please?

Unit 47

1 merrily, prettily, happily, speedily, steadily, hastily, drowsily, wearily, hungrily, lazily, angrily, grumpily noisily, dizzily

2 happiness, loneliness, dizziness, weariness, drowsiness, laziness, cheekiness, fuzziness, shininess, sleepiness, steadiness, liveliness

Unit 48

A	P	R	I	L	F	E	B	R	U	A	R	Y	T
U	U	J	U	M	H	E	N	O	M	A	R	C	H
G	L	G	A	U	T	L	T	R	A	A	R	C	G
U	Y	Y	U	I	N	I	E	N	U	A	R	C	I
S	R	J	U	N	O	B	A	N	D	L	E	A	N
T	A	R	U	N	M	U	A	H	E	N	B	L	T
D	N	E	E	E	A	J	J	A	T	I	M	E	R
E	E	B	V	L	U	C	I	U	T	T	E	N	O
C	T	O	I	L	B	A	R	T	N	O	T	D	F
A	N	T	Y	I	M	Y	W	M	W	E	P	A	W
D	E	C	E	M	B	E	R	J	A	N	E	R	Y
E	C	O	M	I	O	W	N	O	V	E	S	T	I

Unit 49

1 you'd, I'd, we've, doesn't, couldn't, they'll, aren't, you've, she'd, would've, you're, he'd, hadn't, we're, there's, she'll

2 a Here's **b** I'd **c** Lazlo's **d** can't **e** Don't **f** What's

Unit 50

Meat and dairy — steak, chicken, burgers, sausage, veal
Seafood — lobster, salmon, crab, sushi, tuna
Vegetables — tomatoes, corn, carrots, lettuce, broccoli
Fruits — strawberries, oranges, melons, apples, bananas

Unit 51

1 knob, **wrist**, **guess**, dou**b**tful, calm, **guard**, lim**b**, autum**n**, stalk, **knot**, an**s**wer, **hour**, crum**b**, **s**cissors, cupboard

2 wrist, calm, autumn, answer, scissors, knob, hour, crumb, guess, doubtful, guard, cupboard, limb, stalk, knot

Unit 52

b	d	b	t	b	l	e	n	d	m	q	m	b
l	z	z	s	w	b	u	b	l	u	n	t	l
i	s	m	a	z	d	l	z	z	m	b	b	a
s	m	l	l	h	c	b	u	n	y	l	l	n
t	o	b	b	m	m	l	d	r	a	a	d	k
e	o	z	z	l	k	i	k	m	j	c	c	e
r	l	z	l	g	a	n	e	z	m	k	b	t
n	b	b	l	o	n	d	e	d	e	l	a	p
k	b	i	b	e	z	z	e	d	o	m	a	z
p	n	t	a	m	s	z	z	o	l	o	e	z
b	l	i	z	z	a	r	d	r	m	o	t	n
t	a	s	l	b	e	m	m	k	p	b	b	m

Unit 53

1 afternoon, birthday, sunburn, bedroom, yourself, sometimes, somewhere, buttonhole, storeroom, anywhere, shoreline, somebody

2 a somewhere, sometimes, somebody **b** storeroom, bathroom

3 flashlight, nightlight, playground

Unit 54

rice, hall, arm, right, sum, hum, hen, wing, cat, round, sure, all, last, pit

Unit 55

1 receive, see, search, well, connect, minute, bound, brave, prize, plank, creak, scream

2 unload, unkind, unable, untrue, uncommon, unusual, unwell, unhealthy, unlikely, uncertain, unclip, unhook

Unit 56

1 arrows, splashes, alleys, countries, vegetables, coaches, eyewitnesses, leaves, armies

2 doubts, doubted, doubting; annoys, annoyed, annoying, empties, emptied, emptying; wraps, wrapped, wrapping

3 a pour **b** mayor **c** allowed **d** weather **e** threw **f** noisiest **g** swapped **h** supplied **i** arranged **j** careful **k** she'll, here

> **Synonyms** are words with the same or similar meanings.
>
> **Scratch** and **scrape** are synonyms. They have the same meaning.
>
> **Dish** and **plate** are synonyms too.

1 Match the words with their synonyms.

begin	course	~~mistake~~	hurt
tear	bitter	calm	hop	rage	slope

error   ......*mistake*......

commence   ....

slant   ....

path   ....

rip   ....

anger   ....

sour   ....

peaceful   ....

harm   ....

jump   ....

> **Antonyms** are words with opposite meanings.
>
> **High** and **low** are antonyms. They have opposite meanings.
>
> **Expensive** and **cheap** are antonyms too.

2 Match the words with their antonyms.

cruel	silent	hasty	~~first~~	build
smooth	full	waste	forget	tight

last   ....*first*...........

kind   ....

loose   ....

rough   ....

destroy   ....

remember   ....

empty   ....

save   ....

noisy   ....

patient   ....

Present tense verbs	
For verbs ending with "y", add "ing" for actions that are happening **now.**	
play	She's **playing** tennis now.
fly	The kite is **flying** very high.

1   Add "ing" to the following verbs.

spy ....spying.......... stay ....

obey .... marry ....

spray .... stray ....

reply .... fry ....

pray .... bury ....

study .... hurry ....

annoy .... destroy ....

worry .... holiday ....

enjoy .... relay ....

2   Add "ing" to the following verbs.

a   (supply) Jessica and I are ..supplying.. the fruit for the class party.

b   (delay) They are .... the start of the concert because the musicians are late.

c   (hurry) He's .... to school bacause he's late for class.

d   (rely) I am .... on you to do your best.

e   (carry) She's .... her baby because the baby can't walk yet.

f   (display) We are .... art in the library next week.

English has many common letter patterns. Many English words begin with the letter pattern "cr".

1 Circle all the words that begin with the letter pattern "cr".

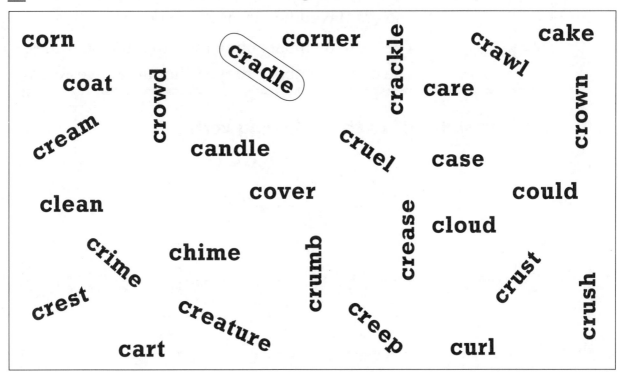

corn   corner   crackle   cake

cradle   crawl

coat   crowd   care   crown

cream   candle   cruel   case

cover   could

clean   cloud

crime   chime   crumb   crease   crust

crest   creature   creep   crush

cart   curl

2 Choose the correct "cr" word to complete the sentences.

crew   crash   cruise   cross   ~~cramped~~   crickets

a It was very...*cramped*.. in the little tent.

b .... can jump a long way.

c There was a loud .... as the tray fell to the floor.

d Last month my family went on a ....

e Be careful when you .... the street.

f The ship has a .... of about 50 members.

Unit 31

Present and past tense verbs	
For verbs ending with a vowel followed by "y", keep the "y" and add "s" or "ed".	
display	She **displays** her art.
	She **displayed** her art at the park.
obey	The crew members **obey** the captain at all times.
	The crew members **obeyed** the captain yesterday.

1 Add "s" and "ed" to the following verbs.

verb	"s"	"ed"
annoy	annoys	annoyed
destroy	....	....
holiday	....	....
relay	....	....
delay	....	....

Present and past tense verbs
When a verb ends in a consonant followed by "y", change the "y" to "i" and add "ed".
copy   **copies / copied**
dry   **dries / dried**

2 Add "es" and "ed" to the following verbs.

verb	"es"	"ed"
dry	dries	dried
tidy	....	....
reply	....	....
study	....	....
empty	....	....
supply	....	....

> **Homophones** are words that sound the same, but have different spellings and different meanings.
>
> flower/flour   The **flower** on her desk is a rose.
>   I need **flour** to bake the cookies.

1   **Choose the correct word to complete the sentences.**

a (shore/sure) I am.......sure...... this is Mario's house.

b (shore/sure) We took a walk along the ....

c (missed/mist) I .... the bus today, so I was late.

d (missed/mist) It wasn't a heavy rain; it was just a light ....

e (plane/plain) I like.................... color clothes–not clothes with dots or stripes.

f (plane/plain) I saw a big .... flying over my house.

g (waist/waste) We are careful not to .... water.

h (waist/waste) The belt was too tight around my ....

i (whether/weather) The forecast is for fine .... tomorrow.

j (whether/weather) I don't know .... I can come to the party.

k (It's/Its) .... my birthday today.

l (it's/its) The dog ate .... food very quickly.

Writing

2   **Rewrite the sentences with all words spelled correctly.**

a We had a grate time at the beach on Thersday.

....

b Adam colected the male from the mailebox.

....

> For most verbs ending with a vowel followed by a consonant, double the consonant to add "ed" and "ing".

| spray | He/She **sprays** | **I sprayed** it yesterday. |
| stay | He/She **stays** | She **stayed** here last night. |

Add "ing" and "ed" to the following verbs.

verb	"ed"	"ing"
grab	*grabbed*	*grabbing*
plan		
strip		
trip		
chop		
chat		
plug		
star		
scrub		
clip		
wrap		
hug		

Measurement word search

Find the measurement words listed in the box. Write the words as you find them.

shape	size	lighter	heavier	balance	kilogram	record
check	centimeter	surface	perimeter	~~boundary~~	capacity	
taller	smaller	column	scale	label	freezing	boiling

m	y	r	a	d	n	u	o	b	m	m	o	z	p
s	i	z	e	m	c	m	o	a	s	c	a	l	e
l	h	m	e	l	o	i	c	l	p	a	s	a	r
c	h	a	m	y	l	j	e	a	t	p	u	q	i
h	e	r	p	i	u	a	n	n	c	a	r	r	m
e	a	u	n	e	m	o	t	c	b	c	f	g	e
c	v	g	e	p	n	m	i	e	e	i	a	t	t
k	i	l	o	g	r	a	m	l	p	t	c	m	e
r	e	t	h	g	i	l	e	a	o	y	e	n	r
l	r	e	c	o	r	d	t	b	j	s	m	l	o
z	m	w	c	r	f	r	e	e	z	i	n	g	v
r	e	l	l	a	m	s	r	l	l	o	m	k	m

............boundary............   ....

....

....

....

....

....

....

....

Add the endings to the following verbs.

verb	"d" or "ed"	"s" or "es"	"ing"
scratch	scratched	scratches	scratching
star			
bury			
decide			
receive			
reply			
plug			
annoy			
waste			
answer			
study			
guess			
clip			
connect			
pedal			

Pedal harder!

English has many common letter patterns. Many English words contain the letter pattern "oi".

1 Circle all the words with the letter pattern "oi".

tone toil rise rose rejoice soak sport

spoil boast boil (moist) coil

join choice coal joke

choke post poison

sole juice oil noisy olive

soil turquoise

recoil turkey nose avoid avid

2 Choose the correct "oi" word to complete the sentences.

voice   coins   point   ~~foiled~~   noise   hoisted

a   The robber was......*foiled*...... by the police.

b   Jess has a nice singing ....

c   The .... of the knife was broken.

d   The .... inside the stadium was very loud.

e   Yuko took the .... out of her purse.

f   The crane .... the heavy load into the air.

Adjectives	
For many words, add "y" to form adjectives.	
salt	**salty**
mess	**messy**

1 Add "y" to the following words.

flour ....*floury*..........   boss ....

butter ....   cream ....

storm ....   fruit ....

oil ....   shadow ....

sugar ....   trick ....

cloud ....   mist ....

For words ending in "e", drop the "e" and add "y" to form adjectives.	
ease	**easy**
shine	**shiny**

2 Add "y" to the following words.

shine ....*shiny*..........   smoke ....

juice ....   scare ....

shade ....   bounce ....

rose ....   wave ....

taste ....   stony ....

nose ....   noise ....

bone ....   stone ....

Exploration word search

Find the exploration words listed in the box. Write the words as you find them.

Europe	explorer	journey	Cook	route
ships	fleet	voyage	~~rations~~	colony
	soldier	transport	England	
	diary	Sydney		

```
Z S E R R O T J A N S Z H C
N K U G L J S H I P S M A O
J C R E R O L P X E W L R N
A O O R O U T E O G H A T V
R L P O M R A T I O N S O I
O O E M K N Z M L E A Y G C
N N J T E E L F N V M D N T
R Y W V O Y A G E C S N D M
E M R E I D L O S O A E I A
V P M P H A J K W M T Y A S
O T R A N S P O R T E D R T
G W P D P H I L L I P I Y S
```

...........rations............   ....

....

....

....

....

....

....

....

Adding "y" and "er"

Adjectives	People
For words ending with a vowel followed by a consonant, double the consonant. Then add "y".	To form words for people who do something, it's the same rule.
run – **runny** chat – **chatty**	run – **runner** trap – **trapper**

1   **Double the final consonant before adding "y" to the words.**

chat   ....*chatty*............   fun   ....

knot   ....   smog   ....

gas   ....   fur   ....

sun   ....   scrub   ....

2   **Double the final consonant before adding "er" to the words.**

swim   ....*swimmer*..........   drum   ....

wrap   ....   snap   ....

plan   ....   stop   ....

hit   ....   tap   ....

cut   ....   win   ....

begin   ....   scan   ....

spin   ....   run   ....

Cities, countries, and continents

New York is a **city.**

France is a **country.**

Africa is a **continent.**

Write the words in the box in the correct list.

Paris   Asia   Italy   ~~Tokyo~~   Seoul   Mexico
North America   Sao Paolo   Canada   Europe   China
South America   Asia   Los Angeles   Thailand

Cities	Countries	Continents
Tokyo	Italy	Asia

Adding "er" and "est"

These are very dry!

Comparatives and superlatives
For adjectives ending with "y", change the "y" to "i" and add "er" or "est".

dry – **drier** – **driest**	fast – **faster** – **fastest**
shady – **shadier** – **shadiest**	slow – **slower** – **slowest**

Add "er" and "est" to the following words.

word	"er"	"est"
shady	shadier	shadiest
dusty		
healthy		
dry		
creamy		
oily		
cloudy		
heavy		
easy		
lively		
smoggy		
noisy		
scary		

Synonyms and antonyms 3

> **Synonyms** are words with the same or similar meanings.
>
> **Begin** and **commence** are synonyms. They have the same meaning.
>
> **Smart** and **intelligent** are synonyms too.

1 Match the words from the box with their synonyms.

castle	knob	guard	~~crush~~	annoy
firm	soil	plot	grab	crawl

squash ....*crush*..........   snatch ....

steady ....   protect ....

plan ....   handle ....

dirt ....   creep ....

fortress ....   bother ....

> **Antonyms** are words with opposite meanings.
>
> **Forget** and **remember** are antonyms. They have opposite meanings.
>
> **Asleep** and **awake** are antonyms too.

2 Match the words from the box with their antonyms.

apart	gain	active	~~sick~~	fancy
many	ugly	lead	commence	always

healthy ....*sick*..........   beautiful ....

together ....   never ....

plain ....   finish ....

lose ....   lazy ....

few ....   follow ....

> **Adverbs**
> Adverbs describe verbs. For many words, add "ly" to form adverbs.
>
> brave – **bravely**   calm – **calmly**

1   Add "ly" to the following words.

calm ....*calmly*..........   sure ....

proud ....   peaceful ....

tight ....   kind ....

hopeful ....   narrow ....

famous ....   final ....

common ....   friend ....

strange ....   pure ....

secret ....   false ....

silent ....   cheaply ....

2   Add "ly" to the following verbs.

a (blind) Daniel and Antonio stumbled ....*blindly*.... around in the dark.

b (smooth) Jackie spread the icing .... over the cake.

c (silent) The children sat ....

d (quiet) Leo walked .... into the room.

e (usual) Joe .... plays soccer on Saturdays.

English has many common letters patterns. Many words contain the letter pattern "ou".

1   Circle all the words with the letter pattern "ou".

stand   sound   loud   soil   oily
early   loan   ground   flour   amount
count   broad   hour   duo   ruin   month
announce   sour   (found)   guard
foreign   clout   pond   pounce   aloud   flood
cute   boat   about   recount

2   Choose the correct "ou" word to complete the sentences.

around   bounced   ~~bound~~   cloud   mouth

a   Min-woo thought the plan was.......*bound*..... to fail.

b   A .... of smoke filled the room.

c   Tim's tooth fell out of his ....

d   Mika turned .... to see who had called her name.

e   The ball .... over the goalie's head.

Using "full"
When adding "full" to the end of a word, drop the last "l".
cheer – **cheerful**   spoon – **spoonful**

1   Add "ful" to the words.

spoon   + full = ...*spoonful*......   pocket + full = ...

waste   + full = ...   success + full = ...

thought + full = ...   delight + full = ...

harm   + full = ...   peace   + full = ...

care   + full = ...   basket   + full = ...

sin   + full = ...   master   + full = ...

rest   + full = ...   youth   + full = ...

doubt   + full = ...   tear   + full = ...

2   Add "full" to the words.

a   (pain) Zac's blistered toe was very ......*painful*....

b   (use) Grandpa found his new tools very ....

c   (help) It's very .... to read the directions before you use the computer.

d   (play) My new kitten is very ....

e   (wonder) "That was a .... movie!" said Pedro.

f   (mouth) Nim couldn't speak because he had a .... of candy.

Homophones are words that sound the same, but have different spellings and different meanings.	
not/knot	We're **not** going there. There's a **knot** in my hair.
hole/whole	There's a **hole** in the wall. I can eat a **whole** pizza.

1 Choose the correct word to complete the sentences.

a (hole/whole) There's a huge ....*hole*........ in my old shirt.

b (hole/whole) I read the .... book in one afternoon.

c (our/hour) It took us an .... to get home.

d (our/hour) We hung .... wet clothes to dry.

e (horse/hoarse) Tadashi voice was .... from shouting.

f (horse/hoarse) Kim rides his .... to school!

g (write/right) We took a .... turn instead of the left.

h (write/right) I don't .... many letters.

i (their/there) .... is no time to lose.

j (their/there) Chung-Ping and Lisa looked at .... new house.

Writing

2 Rewrite the sentences with all words spelled correctly.

a How much is the fair to seoul?

....

b May I have sum ice cream, pleese?

....

Adding "ly" and "ness"

Adverbs and nouns
For adjectives ending in "y", change the "y" to "i" and add "ly" to make an adverb, or add "ness" to make a noun.
easy – **easily**   tidy – **tidiness**

1   Add "ly" to the following words.

merry   ....*merrily*.........   pretty   ....

happy   ....   speedy   ....

steady   ....   hasty   ....

drowsy   ....   weary   ....

hungry   ....   lazy   ....

angry   ....   grumpy   ....

noisy   ....   dizzy   ....

2   Add "ness" to the following words.

happy   ....*happiness*.......   lonely   ....

dizzy   ....   weary   ....

drowsy   ....   lazy   ....

cheeky   ....   fuzzy   ....

shiny   ....   sleepy   ....

steady   ....   lively   ....

Drowsy today ?

Find the time words listed in the box. Write the words as you find them.

January	February	March	April	May	June	July	August

September   October   November   December   month

decade   century   ~~millennium~~   calendar

A	P	R	I	L	F	E	B	R	U	A	R	Y	T
U	U	J	U	M	H	E	N	O	M	A	R	C	H
G	L	G	A	U	T	L	T	R	A	A	R	C	G
U	Y	Y	U	I	N	I	E	N	U	A	R	C	I
S	R	J	U	N	O	B	A	N	D	L	E	A	N
T	A	R	U	N	M	U	A	H	E	N	B	L	T
D	N	E	E	E	A	J	J	A	T	I	M	E	R
E	E	B	V	L	U	C	I	U	T	T	E	N	O
C	T	O	I	L	B	A	R	T	N	O	T	D	F
A	N	T	Y	I	M	Y	W	M	W	E	P	A	W
D	E	C	E	M	B	E	R	J	A	N	E	R	Y
E	C	O	M	I	O	W	N	O	V	E	S	T	I

..............*millennium*..............   ....

....

....

....

....

....

....

....

....

Contractions

I have no idea!

Contractions
has + not = **hasn't**   do + not = **don't**

1   Join the words to form contractions.

you	+	would	=	......*you'd*....	I	+	had	= ....
we	+	have	=	....	does	+	not	= ....
could	+	not	=	....	they	+	will	= ....
are	+	not	=	....	you	+	have	= ....
she	+	had	=	....	would	+	have	= ....
you	+	are	=	....	he	+	had	= ....
had	+	not	=	....	we	+	are	= ....
there	+	is	=	....	she	+	will	= ....

2   Circle the correct contraction.

a	Here is my seat.	(Here's)	Here'is	Heres'
b	I would like to come to the party.	I'ld	Id'	I'd
c	Lazlo has seen that movie already.	Lazlo'has	Lazlo's	Lazlos'
d	Chloe cannot see her father.	cann't	can't	cant'
e	Do not be home late.	Dont	Do'nt	Don't
f	What is the time?	Whats'	What's	Wha'ts

Unit 50

Meat and dairy come from land animals.

Seafood comes from ocean animals.

Vegetables come from plants. They grow out of the ground.

Fruits usually grow from trees.

Write the words in the box in the correct list.

chicken	lobster	strawberries	tomatoes	~~steak~~	oranges
salmon	lettuce	burgers	corn	sausage	crab	melons
veal	sushi	carrots	apples	tuna	broccoli	bananas

Meat and dairy	Seafood	Vegetables	Fruits
steak	lobster	tomatoes	strawberries
....	....	....	....
....	....	....	....
....	....	....	....
....	....	....	....

Unit 51

Silent letters
Many English words contain silent letters.
lam**b** (silent "b")   **k**now (silent "k")

1 **Circle the silent letter in each of the words.**

ⓚnob	wrist	guess	doubtful
calm	guard	limb	autumn
hour	stalk	knot	answer
crumb	scissors	cupboard	

2 **Match the words from Exercise 1 to the meanings below.**

the part of your arm near your hand   ....*wrist*..................

gentle, quiet and still   ....

the season after summer   ....

reply   ....

cutting tools with two blades   ....

a handle on a door   ....

sixty minutes   ....

a tiny piece of bread   ....

to estimate   ....

uncertain   ....

to protect   ....

a place for glasses and cups   ....

an arm or a leg   ....

the stem of a plant   ....

to tie   ....

Unit 52

English has many common letter patterns. Many English words contain the letter pattern "bl".

1 Find the "bl" words listed in the box. Write the words as you find them.

blast	blanket	black	blade	~~blunt~~	blame
bloom	blind	blaze	blend	blizzard	blonde
	blister	blood	blue	blur	

b	d	b	t	b	l	e	n	d	m	q	m	b
l	z	z	s	w	b	u	b	l	u	n	t	l
i	s	m	a	z	d	l	z	z	m	b	b	a
s	m	l	l	h	c	b	u	n	y	l	l	n
t	o	b	b	m	m	l	d	r	a	a	d	k
e	o	z	z	l	k	i	k	m	j	c	c	e
r	l	z	l	g	a	n	e	z	m	k	b	t
n	b	b	l	o	n	d	e	d	e	l	a	p
k	b	l	b	e	z	z	e	d	o	m	a	z
p	n	t	a	m	s	z	z	o	l	o	e	z
b	l	i	z	z	a	r	d	r	m	o	t	n
t	a	s	l	b	e	m	m	k	p	b	b	m

blunt

....

....

....

....

....

....

....

Unit 53

Compound words
Two small words can sometimes form one bigger word.

bath	+ room	=	**bathroom**
flash	+ light	=	**flashlight**
life	+ style	=	**lifestyle**

1 Join the smaller words to form compound words.

after + noon = *afternoon.*   birth + day = ...

sun + burn = ...   bed + room = ...

your + self = ...   some + times = ...

some + where = ...   button + hole = ...

store + room = ...   any + where = ...

shore + line = ...   some + body = ...

2 Use the words in Exercise 1 to answer the following questions.

a Which three compound words contain the word "some"?

....

b Which two compound words contain the word "room"?

....

3 Unjumble the letters and then solve the two compound word sums.

a (fslah) ......*flash*...... + light = *flashlight.*

b (ngiht) .... + light = ...

c (lpya) .... + ground = ...

Unit 54

Small words inside bigger words
ice in **voice**
pot in **potato**
pad and **dock** in **paddock**

Find the smaller words in the words in bold.

Find a grain in **price**. ....*rice*........................

Find a large room in **shall**. ....

Find a part of your body in **farm**. ....

Find correct in **bright**. ....

Find total in **summer**. ....

Find a type of singing in **thumb**. ....

Find a chicken in **kitchen**. ....

Find a part of a bird in **swing**. ....

Find an animal that drinks milk in **catch**. ....

Find a circle in **ground**. ....

Find a word meaning *certain* in **treasure**. ....

Find everyone in **valley**. ....

Find the opposite of *first* in **blast**. ....

Find a hole in the ground in **capita**l. ....

> **Synonyms** are words with the same or
> similar meanings.

> **Answer** and **reply** are synonyms. They have
> the same meaning.
> **Accept** and **receive** are synonyms too.

1 **Match the words with their synonyms.**

| minute   bound   scream   ~~receive~~   prize   see |
| creak   well   search   plank   brave   connect |

accept   .... _receive_ ....   notice   ....

seek   ....   healthy   ....

join   ....   tiny   ....

tied   ....   daring   ....

award   ....   board   ....

squeak   ....   shriek   ....

> **Antonyms** are words with different
> meanings. Some antonyms are formed by
> adding "un" to the beginning of a word.

> **Unwrap** and **wrap** are antonyms. They have
> opposite meanings.
> **Unload** and **load** are antonyms too.

2 **Write the antonyms by adding "un" to the beginning of the
words.**

load   .... _unload_ ....   kind   ....

able   ....   true   ....

common   ....   usual   ....

well   ....   healthy   ....

likely   ....   certain   ....

clip   ....   hook   ....

Spelling test!

1 Write the plurals of these words.

arrow	*arrows*	splash	....	alley	....
country	....	vegetable	....	coach	....
eyewitness	....	leaf	....	army	....

2 Add the endings shown to these words.

	"s" or "es"	"ed"	"ing"
doubt	*doubts*	*doubted*	*doubting*
annoy	....	....	....
empty	....	....	....
wrap	....	....	....

3 Circle the correct word in the brackets.

a Would you please (pour)/poor) the juice?

b The (mayor/mare) spoke to the audience.

c Kana is not (allowed/aloud) to go to the park.

d Tomorrow's (weather/whether) will be warm and sunny.

e Li (through/threw) the ball to me.

f This is the (noisyest/noisiest) class in the school!

g I (swaped/swapped) cards with Yu-mi.

h We (supplied/supplyed) the drinks for the party.

i Yi-Ming and I (arranged/arrangd/arrangeed) to meet after school.

j If you are not (careful/carefull) you will drop the eggs!

k Julia said (she'l/she'll/she'ill) be (hear/here) soon.

OXFORD
UNIVERSITY PRESS

198 Madison Avenue
New York, NY 10016 USA

Great Clarendon Street, Oxford OX2 6DP UK

Oxford University Press is a department of the University of Oxford.
It furthers the University's objective of excellence in research,
scholarship, and education by publishing worldwide in

Oxford   New York

Auckland   Cape Town   Dar es Salaam   Hong Kong   Karachi
Kuala Lumpur   Madrid   Melbourne   Mexico City   Nairobi
New Delhi   Shanghai   Taipei   Toronto

With offices in

Argentina   Austria   Brazil   Chile   Czech Republic   France   Greece
Guatemala   Hungary   Italy   Japan   Poland   Portugal   Singapore
South Korea   Switzerland   Thailand   Turkey   Ukraine   Vietnam

OXFORD and OXFORD ENGLISH are registered trademarks of
Oxford University Press.

© Oxford University Press 2008

Originally published by Oxford University Press Australia in 2005

This edition is adapted by arrangement with Oxford University Press
Australia and licensed for sale in Korea and the rest of the world,
but excluding the US, UK, Australia and New Zealand, and for
export therefrom.

Database right Oxford University Press (maker)

Any websites referred to in this publication are in the public domain
and their addresses are provided by Oxford University Press for
information only. Oxford University Press disclaims any responsibility
for the content.

Market Development Director, Asia: Chris Balderston
Managing Editor, Asia: Barnaby Pelter
Project Manager, Editorial, Production, Design: Allison Harm
Manufacturing Manager: Shanta Persaud
Manufacturing Controller: Eve Wong

ISBN: 978 0 19 478301 9

Printed in China

Printing (last digit) 10   9   8   7   6   5   4   3   2   1

*We would like to thank the following for permission to reproduce the cover
photograph:* World of Stock: Reimar Gaertner (butterfly image).